Kid's Box

New Generation

British English

Caroline Nixon &
Michael Tomlinson

CAMBRIDGE

Pupil's Book
with eBook

1

Language summary

	Key vocabulary	Key language	Sounds and spelling
1 Hello! page 4	**Character names:** Mr Star, Mrs Star, Stella, Simon, Suzy, Marie, Maskman, Monty, Meera **Numbers:** 1–10 **Colours:** blue, green, pink, purple, red, orange, yellow, rainbow	**Greetings:** Hello. Goodbye. **Question words:** What's your name? I'm (Stella). How old are you? I'm (five).	Initial letter sound: '*r*' (<u>r</u>ed)
2 My school page 10	**School:** book, chair, eraser, pen, pencil, table **Character names:** Alex, Lenny	**Question words:** Who's that? That's (Alex). How old is he/she? He's/She's (seven). Is he/she …? Yes, he/she is. No, he/she isn't. How are you? I'm fine, thank you.	Initial letter sounds: '*p*' and '*b*' (<u>p</u>en and <u>b</u>ag)

Marie's art: What happens when you mix colours?   page 16   **Trevor's values:** Make friends   page 17

	Key vocabulary	Key language	Sounds and spelling
3 Favourite toys page 18	**Toys:** ball, bike, car, computer, doll, drum, train **Colours:** black, brown, grey, white	**Question words:** What's your favourite toy? My favourite toy's my (drum). **Prepositions of place:** in, next to, on, under Where's your (ball)? It's (under) the (table). Is (the ball on the chair)? Yes, it is. No, it isn't.	Initial letter sounds: '*t*' and '*d*' (<u>t</u>oy, <u>d</u>oll)
4 My family page 24	**Family:** brother, sister, father, mother, grandfather, grandmother	**Adjectives:** beautiful, happy, sad, old, young He's/She's (happy). We're (young).	Short vowel sound: '*a*' (h<u>a</u>t)

Marie's science: Which planets are near Earth?   page 30   **Trevor's values:** Be kind   page 31

Review: units 1, 2, 3 and 4   page 32

	Key vocabulary	Key language	Sounds and spelling
5 Our pets page 34	**Animals:** bird, cat, dog, fish, horse, mouse	**Adjectives:** big, small, clean, dirty, long, short It's (long). They're (dirty).	Short vowel sound: '*e*' (h<u>e</u>n)
6 My face page 40	**The body and face:** ears, eyes, face, hair, head, knees, mouth, nose, shoulders, toes, tooth/teeth	**Have got for possession:** Have you got (big ears)? Yes, I have. No I haven't. I've got (black hair).	Consonant sounds: '*t*' and '*th*' (<u>t</u>ooth, <u>th</u>ree)

Marie's science: How do we use our senses?   page 46   **Trevor's values:** Look after pets   page 47

1 Hello!

1 🎧 2–3 **Listen and point. Listen and repeat.**

Mr Star

Mrs Star

Simon

Suzy

Stella

2 **Point and say the name.**

Stella

Vocabulary presentation 1: character names | **Language presentation 1:** greetings and question words

1 🎧 4 **Listen and do the actions.**

Maskman   Marie   Monty

2 🎵🎧 5 **Listen and say the chant.**

1 🎧 6 ▶ Listen and point.

2 🎧 7 Listen and repeat.

Vocabulary practice 2: numbers 1–10 | **Language presentation and practice 2:** question words

1  Listen and sing. Do karaoke.

Red and yellow and ⬛ and green.
Orange and purple and 🎨.
I can sing a 🌈.

2 🎧 10 Listen and say the colour.

Monty's sounds and spelling

1 🎧 11 ▶ **Watch and say.**

*A **r**ed **r**obot on a **r**ainbow.*

2 **Look, find and count.**

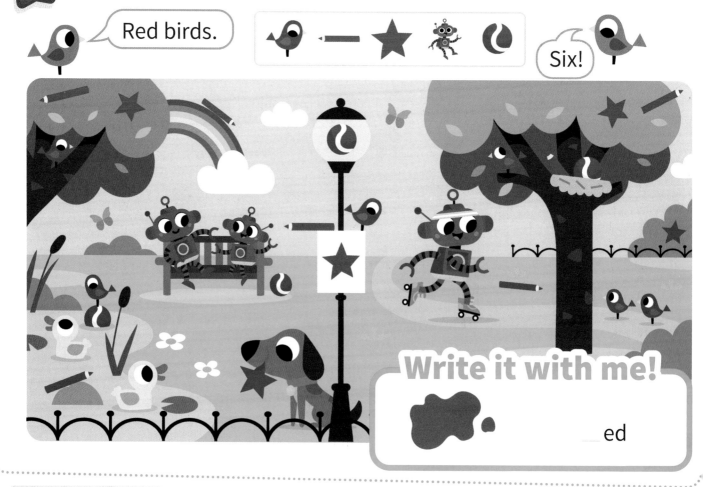

Red birds.

Six!

Write it with me!

ed

1 🎧 12 ▶ **Watch the video.**

 2 **Act out the story.**

2 My school

1 🎧 13-14 **Listen and point.**
Listen and repeat.

chair

chair

table

eraser

pencil

pen

book

2 **Play and say.**   Pen.   It's blue.

Vocabulary presentation: school

1 🎵🎧 15 Listen and say the chant.

A ✏️, a 📕, an ⬜, a ▬,
A 🟦table, a 🪑chair. Say it again!

2 🎧 16 Listen and correct.

Four purple chairs.   No. Six orange chairs.

1 🎧 17–18 ▶ Listen and point. Listen and repeat.

2 Point, ask and answer.

Language presentation and practice 1: question words *Who's that? That's (Lenny). How old is he/she? He's/She's (seven).*

1 ♫🎧 19–20 ▶ Listen and sing. Do karaoke. ②

_____ Star, _____ Star, how are you?
I'm fine, thank you. I'm fine, thank you.
How are you?

Project

Make the puppets.

monty's sounds and spelling

1 🎧 21 ▶ **Watch and say.**

Put the pizza in the purple bag.

2 **Look, point and say.**

Seven pink books.

Write it with me!

ag   izza

1 🎧 22 ▶ Watch the video.

2 Act out the story.

Marie's art

What happens when you mix colours?

1 ▶ **Watch and answer.**

2 🎧 23 **Listen and look. Say the colours.**

Primary colours

Secondary colours

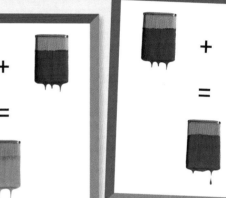

3 **Look, say and tick.**

1   + =   ✓   ☐

2   + =   ☐   ☐

3   + =   ☐   ☐

4 ⚪ + =   ☐   ☐

Red is the first colour a baby can see.

Fact

Project

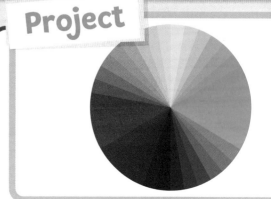

Make a colour wheel.

Trevor's values

Make friends

 1 🎧 24 **Listen and point.**

 2 🎧 25 **Listen and say the number. Act it out.**

3 Favourite toys

1 🎧 26-27 **Listen and point. Listen and repeat.**

doll

drum

computer

car

ball

bike

train

2 **Ask and answer.**

What's this?

It's a car.

1  **Listen and say the chant.**

Black, brown, white, grey.
Look, listen, point and say.

2 🎧 29 **Listen and say the number.**

Is your ball in your bag?

No, it isn't, Dad.

2 **Ask and answer.** Where's your pencil? It's on the table.

1  32-33 ▶ Listen and sing. Do karaoke.

2 Ask and answer.

Is Monty under the chair? No, he isn't.

Language presentation and practice: prepositions of place *Is (Monty) in / on / under / next to the (table)?* **21**

1 🎧 34 ▶ **Watch and say.**

A doll, a drum and a teddy on a train.
Drive under two tables!

2 **Look and say.**

A train on the table.

Number one.

Write it with me!

 able ___ rum

🎧 35 ▶ **Watch the video.**

 🎧 36 **Listen and say 'yes' or 'no'.**

4 My family

grandfather

grandmother

brother

sister

mother

father

2 **Point and say.**

Who's this?

Grandmother!

1 🎧 39 Listen and say the number.

2 🎧 40 Look, listen and say.

ugly

sad

old

happy

young

beautiful

2 Play and say.

You're happy!

Yes!

1  **Listen and sing. Do karaoke.**

2 🎵🎧 45 **Listen and say the chant.**

Language practice 1: adjectives *She's / He's (happy).* 27

1 🎧 46 ▶ **Watch and say.**

A sad cat on a mat. A happy cat in a black hat.

2 **Play and say.**

He's happy. He's next to a hat.

Grandfather!

Write it with me!

h   t

1  Watch the video.

2 Listen and say the number.

Story: unit language in context 29

Marie's science

Which planets are near Earth?

1 ▶ **Watch and answer.**

2 ♪ 49 **Listen, point and say.**

Mercury · Earth · Jupiter · Uranus · The Sun · Venus · Mars · Saturn · Neptune

3 **Colour and say.**

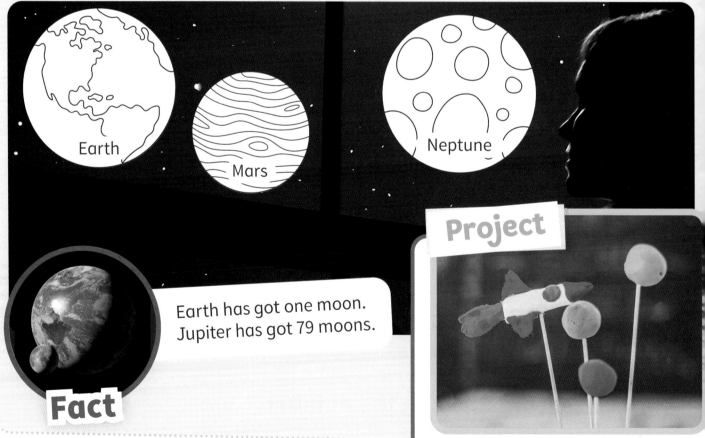

Earth

Mars

Neptune

Earth has got one moon.
Jupiter has got 79 moons.

Fact

Project

Make a planet.

Trevor's values

Be kind

1 🎧 50 **Listen and write the number.**

2 🎧 51 **Listen again and act it out.**

Review Units 1, 2, 3 and 4

 🎧 52 **Listen and say the number.**

2 Say and guess.

> It's pink. It's in a bag.

> Number four.

3 🎧 53 **Listen and colour. Make a spinner.**

  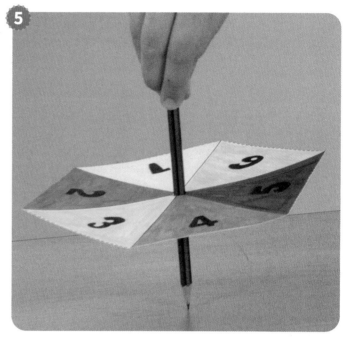

 4 **Play the game.**

5 Our pets

horse

The Star House
PET SHOW

dog

fish

mouse

cat

bird

2 **Say and guess.**   Suzy.   It's a dog.

Vocabulary presentation: animals

 🎵🎧 56 Listen and say the chant.

My horse is beautiful. My dog is too.
My fish is ugly. My bird is blue.

 🎧 57 Listen and say 'yes' or 'no'.

1 🎧 58–59 ▶ Listen and point. Listen and repeat.

dirty

clean

small

long

big

short

2 Ask and answer.

What's long and grey?

The pencil.

Language presentation: adjectives *It's (clean). They're (dirty).*

1 🎵 60 **Listen and do the actions.**

My name's [ ], and this is my [ ].

It's a [ ] [ ]. It's a [ ] [ ].

5

2 🎵🎧 61–62 ▶ **Listen and sing. Do karaoke.**

 **Monty's sounds and spelling**

1 🎧 63 ▶ **Watch and say.**

Ten red pet hens next to a nest!

2 **Ask and answer.**

Where's the pink hen?

It's on the dog.

Write it with me!

h _ n

1 64 ▶ **Watch the video.**

2 **Act out the story.**

Story: unit language in context   39

6 My face

1 🎧 65-66 **Listen and point. Listen and repeat.**

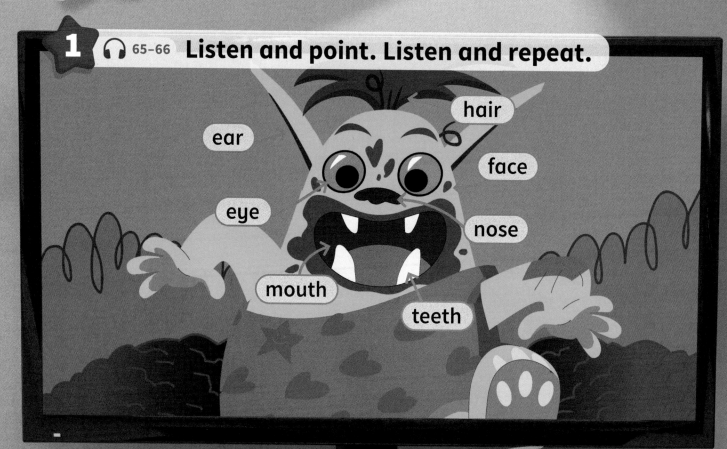

ear

eye

hair

face

nose

mouth

teeth

2 **Play and say.**

Nose.

40   Vocabulary presentation: the face

 🎵🎧 67 Listen and say the chant.

Head, shoulders, knees and toes, knees and toes.

2 🎧 68 Listen and correct.

I'm a boy monster.

No. You're a girl monster.

1 🎧 69–70 ▶ **Listen and point. Listen and repeat.**

2 **Play and say.**

Language presentation 1: have got for possession *Have you got (a small mouth)? I've got (pink hair).*

1  **Listen and sing. Do karaoke.**

I've got ✸ hair, and my ⬤ are red.
I've got a blue 💧, and a ✸ head.

2 **Draw and colour. Say, listen and draw.**

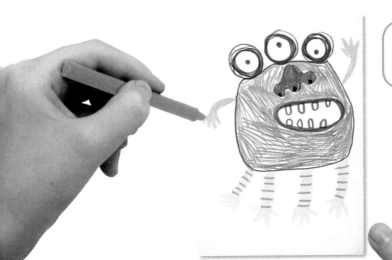

I'm a very ugly monster. I've got three eyes.

Language practice 1: have got for possession *I've got (a purple head).*   43

1 🎧 73 ▶ **Watch and say.**

One **t**oo**th**, **t**wo **t**ee**th**, **th**ree **t**ee**th** in Mrs Mons**t**er's mou**th**.

2 **Say and guess.**

I've got three small teeth.

Monster four!

①

②

③

④

Write it with me!

2 wo   **3** ree

1 🎧 74 ▶ Watch the video.

2 🎧 75 Listen and say 'yes' or 'no'.

Marie's science

How do we use our senses?

1 ▶ **Watch and answer.**

2 🎧 76 **Listen and point.**

3 **Point and say.**

(Eyes.)   (I see with my eyes.)

We taste with our mouth. A butterfly tastes with its feet!

Fact

Project

Use your senses!

Trevor's values

Look after pets

1 🎧 77 **Listen and say the number.**

2 **Do the actions. Guess.**

You feed your fish.   Yes, that's right!

7 Wild animals

1 🎧 78–79 **Listen and point. Listen and repeat.**

bear

giraffe

elephant

snake

crocodile

monkey

hippo

tiger

2 Play and say.

It's big and grey.

It's an elephant!

Vocabulary presentation: animals

1 🎵🎧 80 Listen and say the chant. Do the actions.

Tiger, elephant, hippo, snake,
Giraffe, bear and crocodile.

2 🎧 81 Listen and point. Answer.

1 🎧 82–83 ▶ **Listen and point. Listen and repeat.**

hand

leg

tail

arm

foot

feet

2 **Play and say.** They've got big heads and small ears.

Hippos.

50 Language presentation and practice 1: have got for possession *They've got (short legs). They haven't got (big heads).*

1  84–85 ▶ Listen and sing. Do karaoke.

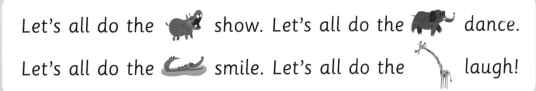

Let's all do the 🦛 show. Let's all do the 🐘 dance.
Let's all do the 🐊 smile. Let's all do the 🦒 laugh!

2 Act it out and say.

> What am I?   You're an elephant.

1 🎧 86 ▶ **Watch and say.**

Six little pink hippos in the river.
He's the big hippo king.

2 **Ask and answer. Guess.**

It's got a long tail.　　A tiger.

Write it with me!

l＿ttle
h＿ppo

1 🎧 87 ▶ Watch the video.

2 Act out the story.

8 My clothes

MASKMAN

cap

skirt

T-shirt

jacket

socks   shoes

trousers   shorts

2 Play and say.   Trousers.   They're grey.

Vocabulary presentation: clothes

1 ♫🎧 90 Listen and say the chant.

I've got blue trousers,
And a green T-shirt.
I've got a brown jacket,
And a purple skirt.

2 🎧 91 Listen and say the number.

Has Simon got my red trousers?

2 **Say and guess.**

She's got white shoes.
She hasn't got blue trousers.

Joana!

Language presentation 1: have got for possession *Have you/Has he/she got (my blue T-shirt)? He/She hasn't got (red shorts).*

 **Listen and correct.**

He's got a 🎨👕 in his hands, a 🎨👕 in his hands.
She's got a 🎨✏️ in her hands, a 🎨✏️ in her hands.

2 🎵🎧 95–96 ▶ **Listen and sing. Do karaoke.**

Language practice 1: have got for possession *She's got (an orange book). He hasn't got (a train).*   **57**

monty's sounds and spelling

1 🎧 97 ▶ **Watch and say.**

Six snakes in T-shirts.

Seven sheep in socks and shoes.

2 **Say and guess.**

They've got red T-shirts.

Monkeys!

Write it with me!

 ___ix ___oes

1 🎧 98 ▶ **Watch the video.**

 🎧 99 **Listen and say the number.**

marie's geography
Where do animals live?

1 ▶ **Watch and answer.**

2 🎧 100 **Listen and match. Write the number.**

1 lion
2 penguin
3 fox
4 polar bear
5 snail
6 bug
7 zebra

1

3 **Look, say and guess.**

It lives in the garden.   A bug.

garden   polar region   savannah

The biggest land mammal is the elephant and it lives in the savannah.

Fact

Project

Make a bird house.

Trevor's values

Love nature

1 🎧 101 **Listen and write the number.**

2 **Mime and guess.**   Plant a tree.   Yes!

Language: *Let's plant a tree. Let's recycle.* | 🛡 social responsibilities   61

🎧 102 **Listen and say the number.**

 Look, read and match. Say. It's a hippo.

polar bear   hippo   zebra   lion

3 **Play and say.**

They're eyes!

Finish

Start

9 Fun time!

1 🎧 103–104 **Listen and point. Listen and repeat.**

play basketball

play the piano

play the guitar

swim

play tennis

play football

ride a bike

2 Play the game.

Simon says…play the piano.

1 🎧 105 **Listen and answer.**

Ride a . Play , basketball.
Play, play, play!
Now let's _____. Play ⚽, the .
Play, play, play!

9

2 🎵🎧 106–107 ▶ **Listen and sing. Do karaoke.**

1 🎧 108–109 ▶ **Listen and point. Listen and repeat.**

I can't sing.

I can ride a bike.

She can ride a horse.

2 Say and guess.

She can't sing.

Stella.

Language presentation 1: can for ability *I/You can (swim). He/She can't (sing).*

1  110 Listen and say the chant.

I can play football, and I can drive my car.
I can't ride a bike, I can't swim.

2 Ask and answer.

Can you ride a bike?   Yes, I can.

Language practice 1: can for ability *Can you (play football)? Yes, I can. No, I can't.*   67

1 🎧 111 ▶ **Watch and say.**

It's a grey day –
snail can play with the train.

2 **Ask and answer.**

What can you do on a grey day?

I can play a game.

Write it with me!

gr_____   sn_____

1 112 ▶ Watch the video.

2 Act out the story.

10 At the funfair

1 🎧 113–114 **Listen and point. Listen and repeat.**

plane

lorry

motorbike

boat

helicopter

bus

2 **Ask and answer.**

Is the lorry blue?

No, it's red.

70 **Vocabulary presentation:** transport

1  115 Listen and say the chant. Do the actions.

Helicopter, ship. Long, blue train.
Motorbike, lorry. Bus and plane.

2 116 Listen and answer.

Is the red car in the shoe?   Yes, it is.

1 🎧 117–118 ▶ **Listen and point. Listen and repeat.**

2 **Play and say.**

Language presentation 1: present continuous (not with future reference) *What are you doing? I'm (riding a bike).*

1  Listen and sing. Do karaoke.

I'm riding on my 🏍️ .
I'm flying in my 🚁 .

2 Do the actions. Ask and answer.

Are you driving a lorry?

No, I'm not.

Are you driving a car?

Yes, I am!

1 121 ▶ **Watch and say.**

Singing a song and swinging along.

Jumping and clapping all day long.

2 **Do the actions. Find and say.**

What am I doing?　　You're singing a song.

Write it with me!

singi____

1 🎧 122 ▶ **Watch the video.**

2 🎧 123 **Listen and say the number.**

Marie's geography

How do we travel?

1 ▶ **Watch and answer.**

2 🎧 124 **Listen and match.**

1 ship
2 monorail
3 hot air balloon

4 scooter
5 van

1

3 **Look and complete.**

| helicopter | scooter | ship | van |
| hot air balloon | monorail |

Air	Road	Rail	Water
plane	car	train	boat

Fact

Some cars can travel on the water.

Project

Design your own transport.

Trevor's values

Work together

1 🎧 125 **Listen and say the number.**

1

2

3

4

2 🎧 126 **Listen and say. Act it out.**

11 Our house

1 🎧 127–128 **Listen and point. Listen and repeat.**

bedroom

bathroom

living room

dining room

kitchen

hall

2 **Ask and answer.**

Who's in the kitchen?

Stella.

1 🎧 129 **Listen and correct.**

Monty's in the bathroom.

No, he isn't.
He's in the bedroom.

2 🎵🎧 130–131 **Listen and answer. Say the chant.**

In the kitchen. In the dining room.
On the bathroom floor.
In the bedroom. In the living room.
Rolling down the hall.

Where's the videogame?

It's in the living room.

He's drawing a picture.

What's Simon doing?

2 **Play and say.**

Stella's riding a bike.

No. She's reading.

1  134–135 ▶ **Listen and sing. Do karaoke.**

Where's [image] ? In her [image].

What's she doing? She's reading a [image].

2 **Ask and answer.**

> What's Stella doing?

> She's reading a book.

> Where is she?

> She's in the bedroom.

1 🎧 136 ▶ **Watch and say.**

> **M**onkey's riding a **m**otorbike in the bedroo**m**.
> **M**ouse is swi**mm**ing in the bathroo**m**.

2 **Ask and answer.**

> Where's Monkey?

> He's in the bathroom.

> What's he doing?

Write it with me!

bedroo

1 🎧 137 ▶ **Watch the video.**

2 🎧 138 **Listen and say 'yes' or 'no'.**

12 Party time!

1 🎧 139–140 Listen and point. Listen and repeat.

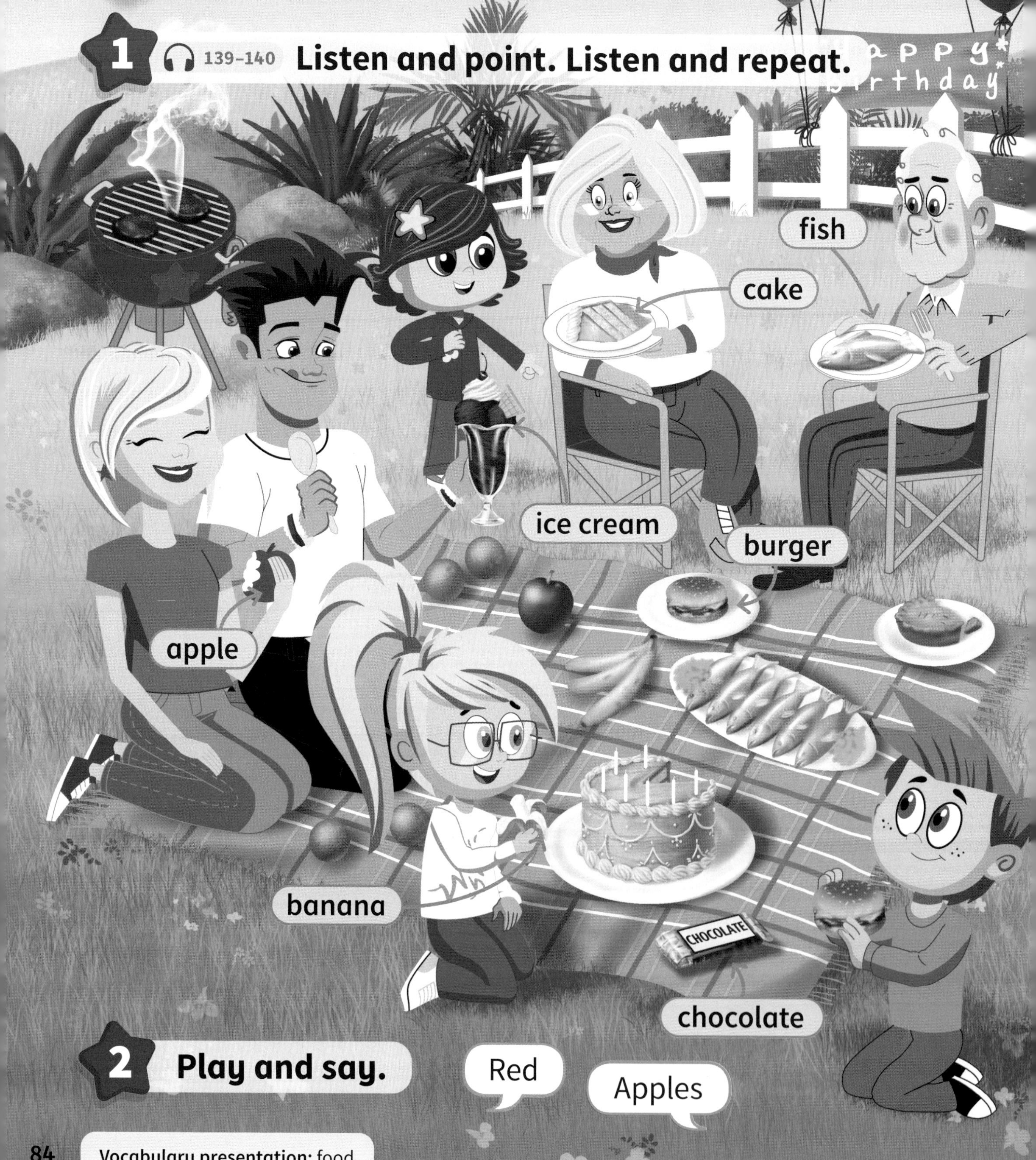

Happy Birthday
fish
cake
ice cream
burger
apple
banana
CHOCOLATE
chocolate

2 Play and say.

Red
Apples

Vocabulary presentation: food

 **1** ♫ 🎧 141 **Listen and say the chant.**

 12

Kiwi and cake.
Ice cream and chocolate.

 **2** 🎧 142 **Listen and say 'yes' or 'no'.**

1 🎧 143–144 ▶ **Listen and point. Listen and repeat.**

I like chocolate cake.

MASKMAN
cake-o-mix

SUGAR

I don't like chocolate.

Do you like Maskman cake?

2 **Play and say.**

I like apples.

I like apples and bananas.

I like apples, bananas and cake.

Language presentation 1: present simple *Do you like (fish)? I like (apples). I don't like (cake).*

1  Listen and sing. Do karaoke.

Do you like 🍌? Yes, yes, yes!

Do you like 🐟? Yes, yes, yes!

Do you like 🍦? Yes, yes, yes!

2 Ask and answer.

Do you like apples?

Yes, I do.

Do you like ice cream?

No, I don't.

Language practice 1: present simple *Do you like (ice cream)? Yes, I do. / No, I don't.* 87

1 🎧 147 ▶ **Watch and say.**

> *Three purple hippos swimming along.*
> *A red snake with big teeth in a hat.*
> *Doll, robot and teddy singing a song.*
> *A boy playing with a mouse, a sheep and a cat.*

2 **Play and say.**

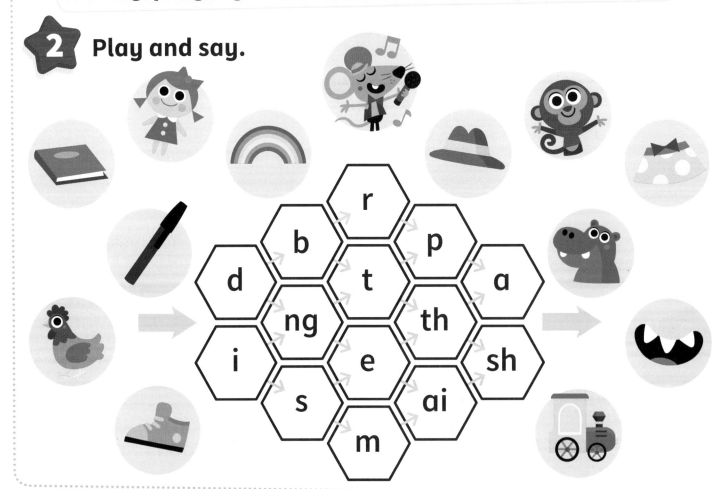

🎧 148 ▶ Watch the video.

2 Act out the story.

Marie's science

How do we grow fruit?

 1 ▶ **Watch and answer.**

 2 🎧 149 **Listen, point and say.**

 3 **Look , complete and say.**

> Apples grow on trees.

> Apples grow in cold places.

Fruit	Tree	Ground	Hot place	Cold place
apples	✓			✓
kiwi				
watermelon				
pear				
strawberries				
orange				

This is called Ugli fruit because it's – ugly!

Fact

Project

Grow fruit.

Trevor's values

Keep clean

1 🎧 150 **Listen and point.**

2 🎵🎧 151 **Listen and say the chant. Do the actions.**

Language: *brush your teeth, wash apples, wash your hands, clean your shoes* | 🛡 social responsibilities

1 🎧 152 Listen and answer.

2 Read.

I'm Ben. I'm **7**. I like ⚽ and 🏐, but I don't like 🏸. I can 🏊 and ride a 🚲, but I can't play the 🎸. I like 🍰 and 🍔, but I don't like 🍫 or 🍦. I like 🍎 and 🥝. I'm eating a 🍌 now.

3 **Play and say.**

They're playing basketball.

Finish

Start

Grammar reference

1

| What's your name? | I'm Suzy. |
| How old are you? | I'm three. |

what's = what is   I'm = I am

2

Who's that?	That's Alex.
How old is he/she?	He's/She's seven.
How are you?	I'm fine, thank you.

who's = who is   that's = that is   he's = he is   she's = she is

3

| Where's your ball? | It's next to the chair. It isn't under the table. |
| Is your ball in your bag? | Yes, it is. No, it isn't. |

where's = where is   it's = it is   isn't = is not

4

| He's happy. | He isn't ugly. |

5

| They're long. | It's dirty. |

they're = they are

6

| I / you / we've got a blue nose. | |
| Have you got a small mouth? | Yes, I have. No, I haven't. |

I've = I have   we've = we have   haven't = have not

7

They've got big heads.	They haven't got long legs.

they've = they have

8

She's got your red trousers.	He hasn't got a blue t-shirt.
Has he got my red trousers?	

hasn't = has not

9

I can ride a bike.	She can't sing.
Can you chant?	

can't = cannot

10

What are you doing?	I'm flying.
Are you riding a bike?	Yes, I am. No, I'm not.

11

What's he doing? What's she doing?	He's drawing a picture She's reading a book.

12

I like chocolate cake.	I don't like chocolate.
Do you like apples?	Yes, I do. No, I don't.

don't = do not

95

Starters Listening

1 🎧 153 **Listen. Who's at school today? Put a tick (✓) or a cross (✗) in the box.**

	📅		📅
Alex	✗	May	
Alice	✓	Nick	
Bill		Lucy	
Grace		Sam	
Kim		Tom	

2 🎧 154 🐵 **Listen and draw lines. There is one example.**

Alex   Sam   Alice   Matt

Kim   Lucy   Eva

Starters Listening

In picture 1, the guitar is next to the bed. In picture 2, the guitar is next to the door.

1 🎧 155 **Look at picture 1 and listen. Say 'yes' or 'no'. Talk about the two pictures.**

2 🎧 156 **Listen and colour. There is one example.**

Starters Reading and Writing

1 **Read and look at your classroom. Say yes or no.**

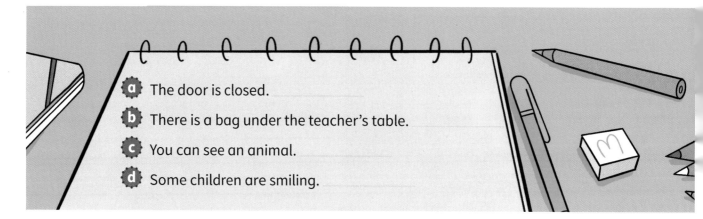

a The door is closed.

b There is a bag under the teacher's table.

c You can see an animal.

d Some children are smiling.

2 **Look and read. Write yes or no.**

Examples

The bedroom door is open.	yes
The boy is smiling.	no

Questions

1 There is a green T-shirt on the chair.

2 The girl has got a bag.

3 The boy is jumping on the bed.

4 The shoes and socks are under the chair.

5 The children are playing tennis.

Starters Reading and Writing

1 🕐 Do the word puzzles. You have 3 minutes!

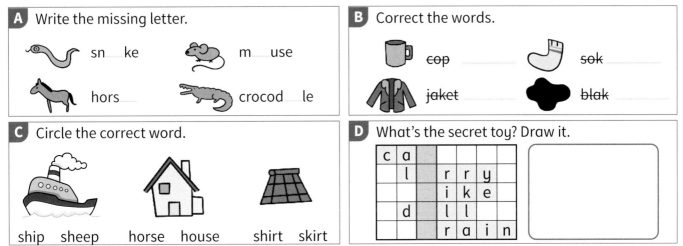

A Write the missing letter.

sn＿ke   m＿use

hors＿   crocod＿le

B Correct the words.

~~cop~~ ＿＿＿＿   ~~sok~~ ＿＿＿＿

~~jaket~~ ＿＿＿＿   ~~blak~~ ＿＿＿＿

C Circle the correct word.

ship sheep   horse house   shirt skirt

D What's the secret toy? Draw it.

c	a				
	l		r	r	y
			i	k	e
	d		l	l	
			r	a	i	n

2 🐵 Look at the pictures. Look at the letters. Write the words.

Example

m o u s e

m
u   e
o   s

Questions

1
n
o   i   l

2
r   i
d
b

3
h   i
p   o
p

4
r   t
e   g   i

5
m   k   n
e   y   o

Starters Speaking

1 **Listen to your teacher. Play the game.**

2 🎧 157 **Listen and draw.**

① ② ③ ④

1 🎧 158 🐵 **Look and listen. Follow the instructions.**

2 🎧 159 🐵 **Listen. Put your cards on the picture.**

3 🎧 160 🐵 **Listen. Answer questions about the zoo.**

Thanks and Acknowledgements

The authors and publishers acknowledge the following sources of copyright material and are grateful for the permissions granted. While every effort has been made, it has not always been possible to identify the sources of all the material used, or to trace all copyright holders. If any omissions are brought to our notice, we will be happy to include the appropriate acknowledgements on reprinting and in the next update to the digital edition, as applicable.

Key: U = Unit

General

Many thanks to everyone at Cambridge University Press and Assessment for their dedication and hard work, and in particular to:
Liane Grainger and Lynn Townsend for supervising the whole project and guiding us calmly through the storms;
Alison Bewsher for her keen editorial eye, enthusiasm and great suggestions;
Zara Hutchinson-Goncalves for her energy, enthusiasm and helpful suggestions.

We would also like to thank all our pupils and colleagues, past, present and future, at Star English academy in Murcia, especially Jim Kelly for his friendship and support throughout the years.

This is for Lydia and Silvia, my own 'Stars', with all my love. – CN

For Paloma, for her love, encouragement and unwavering support. Thanks. – MT

Photography

The following photos are sourced from Getty Images.

U1: Anna Erastova/iStock/Getty Images Plus; **U2:** Dimitri Otis/Stone; legalALIEN/DigitalVision Vectors; Eratel/DigitalVision Vectors; Thoth_Adan/DigitalVision Vectors; Bobby Coutu/E+; LightFieldStudios/iStock/Getty Images Plus; Ariel Skelley/DigitalVision; manonallard/E+; hadynyah/E+; Godruma/iStock/Getty Images Plus; EkaterinaKu/iStock/Getty Images Plus; aldarinho/iStock/Getty Images Plus; Anna Erastova/iStock/Getty Images Plus; **U3:** Anna Erastova/iStock/Getty Images Plus; **U4:** Mark Garlick/Science Photo Library; Samantha T. Photography/Moment; Carol Yepes/Moment; Andersen Ross Photography Inc/DigitalVision; Shingo Tosha/AFLO; Klaus Vedfelt/DigitalVision; picture/iStock/Getty Images Plus; Tim Robberts/DigitalVision; yozachika/iStock/Getty Images Plus; Pongnathee Kluaythong/EyeEm; Nednapa Chumjumpa/EyeEm; FreedomMaster/iStock/Getty Images Plus; broeb/iStock/Getty Images Plus; GlobalStock/E+; Jordan Siemens/Stone; Thomas Barwick/DigitalVision; Stockbyte; skynesher/iStock/Getty Images Plus; Anna Erastova/iStock/Getty Images Plus; **U6:** Jose Luis Pelaez Inc/DigitalVision; Barbara Friedman/Moment; sharply_done/E+; Geri Lavrov/Moment Open; J Shepherd/Photodisc; Lorianne Ende/EyeEm; Jim Cumming/Moment; Mint Images - Jamel Toppin/Mint Images RF; paul mansfield photography/Moment Open; Comstock/Stockbyte; vladans/iStock/Getty Images Plus; kobbydagan/iStock Editorial/Getty Images Plus; **U8:** Ingunn B. Haslekaas/Moment; Achim Mittler, Frankfurt am Main/Moment; Westend61; John Seaton Callahan/Moment; Paul Souders/Stone; Yuriy_Kulik/iStock/Getty Images Plus; Matteo Colombo/Moment; Rosemary Calvert/Stone; goinyk/iStock/Getty Images Plus; Ghislain & Marie David de Lossy/The Image Bank; 35007/E+; DmyTo/iStock/Getty Images Plus; RuslanDashinsky/E+; Jamie Grill/The Image Bank; Jose Luis Pelaez Inc/DigitalVision; Fat Camera/E+; snipes213/iStock/Getty Images Plus; kuritafsheen/RooM; Adam McGrath/500px Prime; David Talukdar/Moment; Leon Woods/EyeEm; Tobias Ackeborn/Moment; JGI; MariaTkach/iStock/Getty Images Plus; Kinwun/iStock/Getty Images Plus; Mike Schultz/EyeEm; RusN/iStock/Getty Images Plus; JackF/iStock/Getty Images Plus; Olga Gillmeister/iStock/Getty Images Plus; DeluXe-PiX/iStock/Getty Images Plus; Aukid Phumsirichat/EyeEm; gofotograf/iStock/Getty Images Plus; Somsak Bumroongwong/EyeEm; Jurmin Tang/EyeEm; ivanastar/E+; Ryan McVay/DigitalVision; GlobalP/iStock/Getty Images Plus; Indeed; heinteh/iStock/Getty Images Plus; amriphoto/E+; Dmytro_Skorobogatov/iStock/Getty Images Plus; hayatikayhan/iStock/Getty Images Plus; Poh Kim Yeoh/EyeEm; Roberto Peradotto/Moment; Morsa Images/DigitalVision; imagenavi; Emely/Cultura; **U10:** Henglein And Steets/Photolibrary; Carl & Ann Purcell/The Image Bank Unreleased; Vacclav/iStock/Getty Images Plus; avid_creative/E+; MichaelSvoboda/iStock/Getty Images Plus; Xuanyu Han/Moment; mikroman6/Moment; prospective56/iStock/Getty Images Plus; Jaris Ho/Moment; AlasdairJames/iStock Unreleased; NathanMarx/E+; monkeybusinessimages/iStock/Getty Images Plus; BJI/Blue Jean Images; Norbert Schaefer/Corbis; SDI Productions/iStock/Getty Images Plus; **U12:** Image Source; Adina Tovy/Lonely Planet Images; Patrick Johns/Corbis/VCG/Corbis Documentary; EdwardSamuelCornwall/iStock/Getty Images Plus; Mr. Patipat Rintharasri/EyeEm; Tom Eversley/EyeEm; Akepong Srichaichana/EyeEm; Creativ Studio Heinemann; Richard Clark/The Image Bank; Anastassios Mentis/Photolibrary; BJI/Blue Jean Images; Dorling Kindersley: Will Heap; vasilis ververidis/500px; Randy Mayor/Photographer's Choice RF; WP Simon/Photodisc; Bignai/iStock/Getty Images Plus; Westend61; zentilia/iStock/Getty Images Plus; rubberball; Jade Albert Studio, Inc./Stone; izusek/E+; ziggy_mars/iStock/Getty Images Plus; Saturated/iStock/Getty Images Plus; Indeed; Image Source/Photodisc; OJO Images/Justin Pumfrey/Photolibrary; NickBiemans/iStock/Getty Images Plus; Meggj/iStock/Getty Images Plus; Torsten Blackwood/AFP; SW Productions/Stockbyte; Tosaphon C/500px Prime; Weedezign/iStock/Getty Images Plus; Delta Images/Image Source.

The following photos are sourced from other libraries.

U2: Gino Santa Maria/Shutterstock; **U12:** Wavebreak Media ltd/Alamy Stock Photo.

Commissioned photography by Copy cat and Trevor Clifford Photography.

Illustrations

Beth Hughes (The Bright Agency); Clara Soriano (The Bright Agency); Gaby Zermeño (Direct artist); Jake McDonald (The Bright Agency); Marek Jagucki (Direct artist); Matthew Scott (The Bright Agency); Pronk Media Inc.

Cover illustration by Pronk Media Inc.

Audio

Audio production by Creative Listening.

Video

Video acknowledgements are in the Teacher Resources on Cambridge One.

Design and typeset

Blooberry Design

Additional authors

Katy Kelly: Monty's Sounds and Spelling
Rebecca Legros: Marie's art, geography and science
Montse Watkin: Exam folder